Especially

....

From

....

Date

....

© 2011 by Barbour Publishing, Inc.

Compiled by Kathy Shutt.

ISBN 978-1-61626-430-7

All rights reserved. No part of this publication may be reproduced or transmitted for commercial purposes, except for brief quotations in printed reviews, without written permission of the publisher.

Churches and other noncommercial interests may reproduce portions of this book without the express written permission of Barbour Publishing, provided that the text does not exceed 500 words or 5 percent of the entire book, whichever is less, and that the text is not material quoted from another publisher. When reproducing text from this book, include the following credit line: *"From Encouraging Words to Live By, published by Barbour Publishing, Inc. Used by permission."*

Scripture quotations marked NIV are taken from the HOLY BIBLE, NEW INTERNATIONAL VERSION®. NIV®. Copyright © 1973, 1978, 1984, 2011 by Biblica, Inc.™ Used by permission. All rights reserved worldwide.

Scripture quotations marked NLT are taken from the *Holy Bible*, New Living Translation, copyright © 1996, 2004, 2007 by Tyndale House foundation. Used by permission of Tyndale House foundation. Carol Stream, Illinois 60188, U.S.A. All rights reserved.

Scripture quotations marked NASB are taken from the New American Standard Bible, © 1960, 1962, 1963, 1968, 1971, 1972, 1973, 1975, 1977, 1995 by The Lockman Foundation. Used by permission.

Scripture quotations marked NCV are taken from the New Century Version of the Bible, copyright © 2005 by Thomas Nelson, Inc. Used by permission.

Published by Barbour Publishing, Inc., P.O. Box 719, Uhrichsville, Ohio 44683, www.barbourbooks.com

Our mission is to publish and distribute inspirational products offering exceptional value and biblical encouragement to the masses.

Printed in China.

Encouraging
Words
to Live By

BARBOUR
PUBLISHING

Believe that life is worth living,
and your belief will help create the fact.

WILLIAM JAMES

Success consists of getting up just
more times than you fall.

OLIVER GOLDSMITH

*I find the great thing in this world
is not so much where we stand,
as in what direction we are moving.
To reach the port of heaven,
we must sail sometimes with the wind and
sometimes against it—but we must sail,
and not drift—nor lie at anchor.*

OLIVER WENDELL HOLMES

I have held many things in my hands and lost them all; but the things I have placed in God's hands, those I always possess.

EARLINE STEELBURG

The happiness of life is made up of minute
fractions—the little soon-forgotten charities
of a kiss, a smile, a kind look, a heartfelt compliment
in the disguise of a playful raillery, and the countless
other infinitesimals of pleasurable thought
and genial feeling.

SAMUEL TAYLOR COLERIDGE

Do not anticipate trouble, or worry about what may never happen. Keep in the sunlight.

BENJAMIN FRANKLIN

Have confidence in God's mercy,
for when you think He is a long way from you,
He is often quite near.

THOMAS À KEMPIS

Character cannot be developed in ease and quiet. Only through experience of trial and suffering can the soul be strengthened, vision cleared, ambition inspired, and success achieved.

HELEN KELLER

There is no impossibility to him who
stands prepared to conquer every hazard.
The fearful are the failing.

SARAH J. HALE

Hope means hoping when things are hopeless,
or it is no virtue at all. . . . As long as matters are
really hopeful, hope is mere flattery or platitude;
it is only when everything is hopeless that
hope begins to be a strength.

G. K. CHESTERTON

"*With God all things are possible.*"

MATTHEW 19:26 NIV

All God's glory and beauty come from within,
and there He delights to dwell.
His visits there are frequent,
His conversation sweet,
His comforts refreshing,
His peace passing all understanding.

THOMAS À KEMPIS

We grow great by dreams. . . . [We] see things in the soft haze of a spring day or in the red fire of a long winter's evening. Some of us let these dreams die, but others nourish and protect them; nurse them through the bad days till they bring them to the sunshine and light which comes always to those who sincerely hope that their dreams will come true.

WOODROW WILSON

I believe that any man's life will be filled with constant and unexpected encouragement if he makes up his mind to do his level best each day, and as nearly as possible reaching the high water mark of pure and useful living.

BOOKER T. WASHINGTON

Life is made up of choices, not chances.
It is up to you to make the right choices
for your life.

CONOVER SWOFFORD

*Dear Lord, hold my hand when
fear threatens to overwhelm and disable me.
When I feel inadequate, insignificant,
or discouraged, give me strength to keep going,
the courage to stand up for what I believe in,
and a desire to give You nothing less than my
very best. Give me faith that conquers fear.*

JENNA MILLER

Don't wait for your ship to come in;
swim out to it.

ANONYMOUS

How far you go in life depends on your being
tender with the young, compassionate with the aged,
sympathetic with the striving, and tolerant of the
weak and the strong. Because someday in life
you will have been all of these.

GEORGE WASHINGTON CARVER

*He who asks a question
is a fool for five minutes;
he who does not ask a question
remains a fool forever.*

CHINESE PROVERB

*Choose always the way that seems best,
however rough it may be.*

PYTHAGORAS

A burden, even a small one, when carried alone
and in isolation can destroy us; but a burden when
carried as part of God's burden can lead us to new
life. That is the great mystery of our faith.

HENRI NOUWEN

Wake each morning with a sense of hope.
God has amazing things in store for you.
And He does all things well.

ELLYN SANNA

*What would life be if we had
no courage to attempt anything?*

VINCENT VAN GOGH

*Keep your face upturned to [God]
as the flowers do the sun.
Look, and your soul shall live and grow.*

HANNAH WHITALL SMITH

When we take time to notice the simple things in life, we never lack for encouragement. We discover we are surrounded by limitless hope that's just wearing everyday clothes.

ANONYMOUS

"For I know the plans I have for you," declares the LORD, *"plans to prosper you and not to harm you, plans to give you hope and a future."*

JEREMIAH 29:11 NIV

*The best way to cheer yourself up is
to try to cheer someone else up.*

MARK TWAIN

*Determine that the thing can and shall be done,
and then we shall find the way.*

ABRAHAM LINCOLN

Help me spread my fragrance everywhere I go.
Flood my spirit with Thy spirit and life.
Penetrate and possess my whole being so utterly
that all my life may only be a radiance of Thine.

JOHN HENRY NEWMAN

Late, have I loved You,
O beauty so ancient and so new.
Late have I loved You!
You were within me while
I have gone outside to seek You.
Unlovely myself, I rushed towards
all those lovely things You had made.
And always You were with me.

AUGUSTINE

God's ways seem dark, but soon or late,
they touch the shining hills of day.

JOHN GREENLEAF WHITTIER

No winter lasts forever;
no spring skips its turn.

HAL BORLAND

*We are so preciously loved by God
that we cannot even comprehend it.
No created being can ever know how much and
how sweetly and tenderly God loves them.*

JULIAN OF NORWICH

Never think that God's delays are God's denials.
Hold on; hold fast; hold out. Patience is genius.

GEORGES-LOUIS LECLERC DE BUFFON

Optimism is the faith that leads to achievement.
Nothing can be done without hope or confidence.

HELEN KELLER

Of all the forces that make for a better world,
none is so indispensable, none so powerful, as hope.

CHARLES SAWYER

*The smallest bit of obedience opens heaven,
and the deepest truths of God
immediately become ours.*

OSWALD CHAMBERS

Communion with God is a great sea that fits every bend in the shore of human need.

HARRY EMERSON FOSDICK

It seems to me that we can never give up
longing and wishing while we are alive.
There are certain things we feel to be
beautiful and good, and we must hunger for them.

GEORGE ELIOT

God's care for us is more watchful and more tender
than the care of any human father could possibly be.

HANNAH WHITALL SMITH

*So, my dear brothers and sisters,
be strong and immovable. Always work
enthusiastically for the Lord, for you know that
nothing you do for the Lord is ever useless.*

1 CORINTHIANS 15:58 NLT

"But" is a fence over which few leap.

GERMAN PROVERB

All dreams can come true—
if we have the courage to pursue them.

WALT DISNEY

Take time to determine the way you will live your life. But once you know the way you should go, let nothing distract you from your path.

ELLYN SANNA

Most people never run far enough on their first wind to find out if they've got a second. Give your dreams all you've got, and you'll be amazed at the energy that comes out of you.

WILLIAM JAMES

Aim high.
Shoot for the stars.
Don't settle for anything less than your best.

ELLYN SANNA

Just waiting for the Lord
to work is often hard to do.
But we must wait for His good time.
He knows what's best for you.

CONOVER SWOFFORD

Why not go out on a limb?
Isn't that where the fruit is?

FRANK SCULLY

All life is an experiment.
The more experiments you make, the better.

RALPH WALDO EMERSON

*Why should we be in such a desperate haste
to succeed, and in such desperate enterprises?
If a man does not keep pace with his companions,
perhaps it is because he hears a different drummer.*

HENRY DAVID THOREAU

Never part with your illusions.
Without dreams you may continue to exist,
but you have ceased to live.

MARK TWAIN

God does not demand the impossible,
but He tells us to do what we can and to ask
for what we cannot do; then He helps us to be able.

COUNCIL OF TRENT

Nobody trips over the mountains.
It is the small pebble that causes you to stumble.
Pass all the pebbles in your path and you will
find you have crossed the mountain.

ANONYMOUS

You gain strength, courage, and confidence by every experience in which you really stop to look fear in the face. You are able to say to yourself, "I have lived through this horror. I can take the next thing that comes along." . . .
You must do the next thing you think you cannot do.

ELEANOR ROOSEVELT

Life is not easy for any of us. But what of that?
We must have perseverance and
above all confidence in ourselves.
We must believe that we are gifted for something
and that this thing must be attained.

MARIE CURIE

We must not become tired of doing good.
We will receive our harvest of eternal life at
the right time if we do not give up.

GALATIANS 6:9 NCV

*The supreme happiness of life
is in the conviction that we are loved;
loved for ourselves, or rather, in spite of ourselves.*

VICTOR HUGO

*There are high spots in all of our lives
and most of them have come about through
encouragement from someone else.*

<small>GEORGE MATTHEW ADAMS</small>

Instruction does much,
but encouragement does everything.

JOHANN WOLFGANG VON GOETHE

When we do the best that we can,
we never know what miracle is wrought in our life,
or in the life of another.

HELEN KELLER

When you get to the end of your rope,
tie a knot and hang on.

FRANKLIN D. ROOSEVELT

A word of encouragement during a failure is worth more than an hour of praise after success.

ANONYMOUS

There is no failure except in no longer trying.

ELBERT HUBBARD

Flatter me, and I may not believe you.
Criticize me, and I may not like you.
Ignore me, and I may not forgive you.
Encourage me, and I may not forget you.

WILLIAM ARTHUR

*Everything that we call a trial,
a sorrow, or a duty, believe me,
that an angel's hand is there.*

Fra Giovanni

When you get in a tight place
and everything goes against you,
until it seems as if you could not hold on
a minute longer, never give up then, for that is
just the place and time when the tide will turn.

HARRIET BEECHER STOWE

All progress occurs because
people dare to be different.

HARRY MILLNER

The will to win, the desire to succeed,
the urge to reach your full potential. . .
these are the keys that will unlock the door
to personal excellence.

EDDIE ROBINSON

*I don't know what your destiny will be,
but one thing I know: The only ones among you
who will be really happy are those who
sought and found how to serve.*

DR. ALBERT SCHWEITZER

*Look at life through the windshield,
not the rearview mirror.*

BRYD BAGGETT

*Such things were written in the Scriptures long ago
to teach us. And the Scriptures give us hope
and encouragement as we wait patiently
for God's promises to be fulfilled.*

ROMANS 15:4 NLT

What you achieve through the journey of life
is not as important as who you become.

ANONYMOUS

*The future belongs to those who believe
in the beauty of their dreams.*

ELEANOR ROOSEVELT

Dear Lord, in my quest for success and accomplishment, help me to remember that to truly be successful, I need to develop the ability to learn from my mistakes, be a servant to others, and put my best efforts into whatever I do.

JENNA MILLER

Be decisive. Don't be afraid to do wrong.
We all make mistakes,
but you'll never accomplish anything
if you never act at all.

ELLYN SANNA

The important thing is not to stop questioning.

ALBERT EINSTEIN

Success is measured not so much by the position that one has reached in life as by the obstacles which he has overcome trying to succeed.

BOOKER T. WASHINGTON

*Do a little more each day
than you think you possibly can.*

LOWELL THOMAS

Oh, the thinks you can think.
If only you try!

Dr. Seuss

This above all: To thine own self be true:
And it must follow, as the night the day,
Thou canst not then be false to any man.

WILLIAM SHAKESPEARE

Everyone has talent.
What is rare is the courage
to follow that talent. . .where it leads.

ERICA JONG

This is my parting word:
Know what you want to do—then do it!

ERNEST SCHUMANN-HEINK

Hide not your talents.
They for use were made.
What's a sundial in the shade?

Benjamin Franklin

The best path to follow through life
is to step in the footsteps of Jesus.

CONOVER SWOFFORD

If Columbus had turned back,
no one would have blamed him.
Of course, no one would have
remembered him either.

ANONYMOUS

For momentary, light affliction is producing for us an eternal weight of glory far beyond all comparison.

2 CORINTHIANS 4:17 NASB

I never did anything worth doing by accident,
nor did any of my inventions come by accident;
they came by work.

THOMAS EDISON

Keep away from people
who try to belittle your ambitions.
Small people always do that, but the really great
make you feel that you, too, can become great.

MARK TWAIN

To become truly great,
one has to stand with people,
not above them.

CHARLES DE MONTESQUIEU

Nothing ever great in the world has ever been accomplished without passion.

HEBBEL

Trials. . .may come in abundance.
But they cannot penetrate into the sanctuary
of the soul when it is settled in God,
and we may dwell in perfect peace.

HANNAH WHITALL SMITH

Be such a person, and live such a life,
that if everyone were such as you,
and every life a life such as yours,
this earth would be God's paradise.

PHILLIPS BROOKS

*I still find each day too short for all the thoughts
I want to think, all the walks I want to take,
all the books I want to read, and all the friends
I want to see. The longer I live,
the more my mind dwells upon the beauty
and wonder of the world.*

JOHN BURROUGHS

Hope is the feeling we have that the feeling we have is not permanent.

MIGNON MCLAUGHLIN

Everything that is done in the world
is done by hope.

MARTIN LUTHER

Throw your heart out in front of you
and run ahead to catch it.

ARABIAN PROVERB

The page of life that had spread out before me was dull and commonplace only because I had not fathomed its deeper import.

NATHANIEL HAWTHORNE

You will find, as you look back upon your life,
that the moments when you have really lived are
the moments when you have done things
in the spirit of love.

HENRY DRUMMOND

The most precious things in life are near at hand.

JOHN BURROUGHS

Never talk defeat;
use words like hope, belief, faith, victory.

NORMAN VINCENT PEALE

*I can do all things through Christ,
because he gives me strength.*

PHILIPPIANS 4:13 NCV

Some people come into our lives and quickly go.
Some stay awhile and leave footprints on our hearts,
and we are never, ever the same.

FLAVIA WEEDEN

*The happiest moments of my life have been
the few which I have passed at home
in the bosom of my family.*

THOMAS JEFFERSON

Hope springs eternal in the human breast.

ALEXANDER POPE

If one advances confidently in the direction
of his dreams, and endeavors to live the life
which he has imagined, he will meet with
a success unexpected in common hours.

ROBERT LOUIS STEVENSON

Trust in the Redeemer's strength. . .
exercise what faith you have, and by and by
He shall rise upon you with healing beneath
His wings. Go from faith to faith and
you will receive blessing upon blessing.

CHARLES H. SPURGEON

Only a life lived for others is worth living.

ALBERT EINSTEIN

To give without any reward, or any notice,
has a special quality of its own.

ANNE MORROW LINDBERGH

*Happiness consists more in small conveniences
or pleasures that occur every day than in
great pieces of good fortune.*

BENJAMIN FRANKLIN

When God shuts a door,
He opens a window.

JOHN RUSKIN

Be on the lookout for mercies.
The more we look for them,
the more of them we will see.
Blessings brighten when we count them.

MALTBIE D. BABCOCK

Your greatest pleasure is that which rebounds
from hearts that you have made glad.

HENRY WARD BEECHER

*This world, after all our science and sciences,
is still a miracle; wonderful, inscrutable
magical, and more.*

THOMAS CARLYLE

This life is not all.
It is an "unfinished symphony"...
with him who knows that he is related to God
and has felt the "power of an endless life."

HENRY WARD BEECHER

Troubles are often the tools by which
God fashions us for better things.

HENRY WARD BEECHER

*Love does not delight in evil
but rejoices with the truth.
It always protects, always trusts,
always hopes, always perseveres.*

1 Corinthians 13:6–7 NIV

The riches that are in the heart cannot be stolen.

RUSSIAN PROVERB

Truth is the beginning of every good thing
both in heaven and on earth.

PLATO

Pray to God, but keep rowing to shore.

RUSSIAN PROVERB

The noblest question in the world is,
"What good may I do in it?"

Benjamin Franklin

Doubt sees the obstacles;
Faith sees the way.
Doubt sees the darkest night;
Faith sees the day.
Doubt dreads to take a step;
Faith soars on high.
Doubt questions, "Who believes?";
Faith answers, "I."

ANONYMOUS

*The secret to success is to do
the common things uncommonly well.*

JOHN D. ROCKEFELLER JR.

Life is like a baseball game.
You do not have to succeed seven out of ten times,
and you can still make the all-star team.

ANONYMOUS

Two roads diverged in a wood and I—
I took the one less traveled by,
And that has made all the difference.

ROBERT FROST

Vision is the art of seeing things invisible.

JONATHAN SWIFT

Use the talents you possess;
the wood would be very silent if no birds sang
except for those that sang best.

HENRY VAN DYKE

It is a mistaken idea that greatness
and great success mean the same thing.

ANONYMOUS

What I must do is all that concerns me,
not what the people think.

RALPH WALDO EMERSON

*Every person you meet
knows something you don't.
Learn from them.*

H. JACKSON BROWN

"Begin at the beginning,"
the king said, gravely,
"and go on till you come to
the end; then stop."

LEWIS CARROLL,
FROM *ALICE IN WONDERLAND*

*Patience and encouragement. . .
come from God.*

ROMANS 15:5 NCV

The greatest satisfaction in life is achieving
what everyone said could not be done.

CHINESE PROVERB

Never mistake motion for action.

ERNEST HEMINGWAY

Wisdom is knowing what to do next.
Skill is knowing how to do it.
Virtue is doing it.

THOMAS JEFFERSON

You may be disappointed if you fail;
but you are doomed if you don't try.

BEVERLY SILLS

So amid the conflict whether great or small,
Do not be disheartened, God is over all;
Count your many blessings, angels will attend,
Help and comfort give you to your journey's end.

JOHNSON OATMAN JR.

Every calling is great when greatly pursued.

OLIVER WENDELL HOLMES

*If we had no winter,
the spring would not be so pleasant;
if we did not sometimes taste adversity,
prosperity would not be so welcome.*

ANNE BRADSTREET

When it is dark enough,
you can see the stars.

CHARLES BEARD

Without sweat and toil
no work is made perfect.

LATIN PROVERB

We learn wisdom from failure
much more than success.
We often discover what we will do,
by finding out what we will not do.

SAMUEL MILLS

*Let no one ever come to you
without leaving better and happier.
Be the living expression of God's kindness:
kindness in your face, kindness in your eyes,
kindness in your smile.*

MOTHER TERESA

Success is the sum of small efforts,
repeated day in and day out.

ROBERT COLLIER

Note how good you feel after
you have encouraged someone else.
No other argument is necessary to suggest
that you should never miss the opportunity
to give encouragement.

GEORGE M. ADAMS

Yes, you can be a dreamer and a doer, too, if you will remove one word from your vocabulary: impossible.

ROBERT SCHULLER

*But, Lord, you are my shield,
my wonderful God who gives me courage.*

PSALM 3:3 NCV

Change is difficult but often essential to survival.

LES BROWN

No one can excel in everything.
The decades demand decisions.
Choose wisely.

PATRICIA SOUDER

The only real failure is to quit.

ANONYMOUS

You cannot discover new oceans
unless you have the courage to
lose sight of the shore.

ANONYMOUS

Self-confidence is the first requisite
to great undertakings.

DR. SAMUEL JOHNSON

Always be a first-rate version of yourself,
instead of a second-rate version of somebody else.

JUDY GARLAND

God gave us two ends—
one to sit on and one to think with.
Success depends on which one you use;
heads, you win—tails, you lose.

ANONYMOUS

The first step toward change is awareness.
The second step is acceptance.

NATHANIEL BRANDEN

To be what we are, and to become what we are
capable of becoming, is the only end of life.

ROBERT LOUIS STEVENSON

A champion is someone who
gets up even when he can't.

ANONYMOUS

Be not afraid of growing slowly;
be afraid only of standing still.

CHINESE PROVERB

Be great in little things.

FRANCIS XAVIER

Light tomorrow with today!

ELIZABETH BARRETT BROWNING

Most of the important things in the world
have been accomplished by people who have kept
on trying when there seemed to be no hope at all.

DALE CARNEGIE

There is no God like you. You forgive those who
are guilty of sin; you don't look at the sins
of your people who are left alive. You will not
stay angry forever, because you enjoy being kind.
You will have mercy on us again; you will
conquer our sins. You will throw away
all our sins into the deepest part of the sea.

MICAH 7:18–19 NCV

God's fingers can touch nothing
but to mold it into loveliness.

GEORGE MACDONALD

It is wonderful what miracles God works
in wills that are utterly surrendered to Him.
He turns hard things into easy,
and bitter things into sweet.
It is not that He puts easy things
in the place of the hard,
but He actually changes the hard thing
into an easy one.

HANNAH WHITALL SMITH

Every heart that has beat strong and cheerfully has
left a hopeful impulse behind it in the world,
and bettered the tradition of mankind.

ROBERT LOUIS STEVENSON

What lies behind us and what lies before us are tiny matters compared to what lies within us.

RALPH WALDO EMERSON

Communication with God is a great sea that fits every bend in the shore of human need.

HARRY EMERSON FOSDICK

I think these difficult times have helped me
to understand better than before how
infinitely rich and beautiful life is in every way
and that so many things that one goes around
worrying about are of no importance whatsoever.

Isak Dinesen

An infinite God can give all of Himself to each
of His children. He does not distribute Himself that
each may have a part, but to each one He gives all
of Himself as fully as if there were no others.

A. W. TOZER

*When everything seems to be going against you,
remember that the airplane takes off
against the wind, not with it.*

HENRY FORD

*Jesus is the Light of the World. . .
the lighthouse that draws us
toward the hope of heaven.*

HOLLEY ARMSTRONG

The LORD hears his people
when they call to him for help.
He rescues them from all their troubles.

PSALM 34:17 NLT